REVIEW COPY NOT FOR RESALE

A Robbie Reader

FROGS IN DANGER

Jim Whiting

Mitchell Lane
PUBLISHERS

P.O. Box 196
Hockessin, Delaware 19707
Visit us on the web: www.mitchelllane.com
Comments? email us: mitchelllane@mitchelllane.com

Printing   1   2   3   4   5   6   7   8   9

A Robbie Reader/On the Verge of Extinction: Crisis in the Environment

Whiting, Jim, 1943-
  Frogs in danger / by Jim Whiting.
      p. cm.—(A Robbie reader)
  Includes bibliographical references and index.
  ISBN-13: 978-1-58415-585-0 (library bound)
  1. Frogs—Juvenile literature. I. Title.
  QL668.E2W485 2007
  597.8'9--dc22
                                                          2007000802

ABOUT THE AUTHOR: Jim Whiting has been a remarkably versatile and accomplished journalist, writer, editor, and photographer for more than 30 years. A voracious reader since early childhood, Mr. Whiting has written and edited about 200 nonfiction children's books on a wide range of topics. From the time he raised tadpoles into frogs at the age of eight, Mr. Whiting has had a keen interest in the natural world. He lives in Washington state with his wife and two teenage sons.

PHOTO CREDITS: p. 4 Getty Images; p. 6 Photo Researchers; p. 10 Dr. Paul A. Zahl/Photo Researchers; p. 20: D. G. Mulcahy. Remaining photographs © 2008 JupiterImages Corporation.

PLB

TABLE OF CONTENTS

Words in **bold** type can be found in the glossary.

EXTINCTION

Four of these frogs are deformed—three in the bottom half of the photo and the one at the top. The other two are normal. When deformed frogs are found, people know there is something wrong in the environment.

Chapter One

FROGS IN TROUBLE

Scientists are very worried about frogs. In the mid-1990s, schoolchildren in Minnesota found frogs that had extra hind legs. Other frogs had only one leg. One frog even had an eye growing inside its throat. Those frogs didn't live very long.

Frogs are very sensitive to their environment. Unhealthy frogs often provide an early warning that something is wrong. Around the world, many frogs have become unhealthy. Some kinds of frogs have become **extinct** (ek-STINKT) in the last few years. That means there are no more of those frogs living in the world. Many other types of frogs are **endangered**. There are very few of them left. They could soon become extinct.

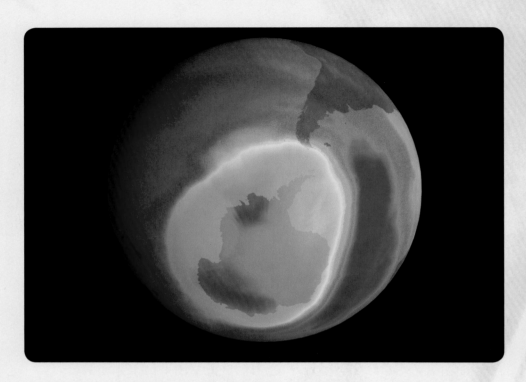

A colored satellite map shows the amount of ozone in Earth's atmosphere. In the green area, called a hole, ozone levels are very low. The hole is over Antarctica.

Scientists believe there are several reasons why frogs have become deformed or have died out completely. Frogs breathe mainly through their skin, which is very thin. Their bodies are sensitive to pollution, **habitat** (HAA-bih-tat) destruction, and climate change.

One cause of climate change is global warming. *Global warming* means the temperature on Earth's surface is increasing. Although Earth's temperature has gone up and down many times in the past, one thing is different now. The temperature is changing much faster than ever before. In the past, creatures had a long time to **adapt** to these changes. Now the changes happen too quickly and creatures can't adapt fast enough.

Earth's **atmosphere** (AT-mus-feer) absorbs heat from the sun's rays. Much of this heat bounces back into space, but the gases in the atmosphere trap some of it. The trapped heat keeps Earth warm enough to sustain life.

One of the most important of these heat-trapping gases is **carbon dioxide** (KAR-bun dy-OCK-syd). Too much carbon dioxide in the atmosphere will cause Earth to be too warm. Burning **fossil fuels** (FAH-sul fyools) such as oil produces higher levels of carbon dioxide.

Chopping down forests also increases the amount of this gas. Trees take in carbon dioxide and give off oxygen (OCK-seh-jun). Oxygen is the gas that people and other animals need to breathe. When people chop down too many trees, there is more carbon dioxide in the atmosphere. There is also less oxygen to breathe.

Trees are helpful in fighting global warming. They reduce the amount of carbon dioxide in the atmosphere. Sometimes too many are cut down in the same area. This is called deforestation.

Red-eyed tree frogs live in South America and Central America. Their bright red eyes can scare away predators. They are losing their habitat to deforestation.

Scientists believe that the increase in carbon dioxide causes higher temperatures on Earth. They are worried that this upward trend will continue. They are keeping track of how these changes affect animals such as frogs.

EXTINCTION

Harlequin frogs in Costa Rica began to die off rapidly in the 1980s. Scientists worked to solve the mystery of why they were disappearing.

IS GLOBAL WARMING TO BLAME?

Scientists began studying the connection between global warming and frogs in the late 1980s. Dozens of kinds of harlequin (HAR-luh-kwen) frogs were disappearing. The frogs lived in the mountains of Costa Rica. Costa Rica is a country in Central America.

Led by J. Alan Pounds, scientists began their research. They wanted to learn why the frogs had disappeared. Early in 2006, Pounds wrote an article about what he had found.

He blamed global warming. He said that hotter temperatures created a dense cloud cover over the mountains. The clouds caused daytime temperatures to drop. They also made nighttime temperatures higher. These temperature changes did not directly affect

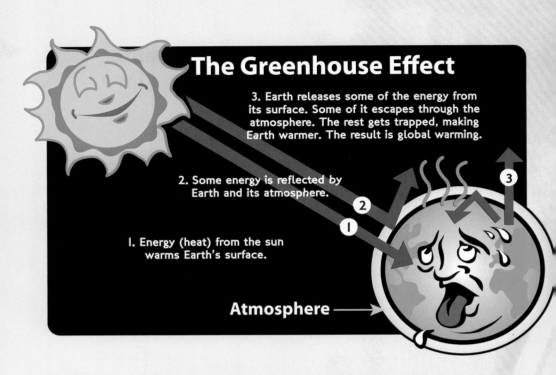

The Greenhouse Effect

3. Earth releases some of the energy from its surface. Some of it escapes through the atmosphere. The rest gets trapped, making Earth warmer. The result is global warming.

2. Some energy is reflected by Earth and its atmosphere.

1. Energy (heat) from the sun warms Earth's surface.

Atmosphere ⟶

The sun warms Earth's surface, and the atmosphere traps the heat to keep the planet at a certain temperature. This is called the greenhouse effect. Global warming happens when extra carbon dioxide in the atmosphere traps too much heat.

the frogs, but they helped the chytrid (KYE-trud) **fungus** to grow.

A fungus feeds by attaching itself to something else. It is easy for this fungus to live on the thin skin of frogs. The fungus makes the frogs lose their skin in layers. In less than two weeks, the frogs die.

The green tree frog is found in Washington State. Its habitat is being destroyed by humans who are building new homes around the regions in which these frogs live. The wetlands, another home for these frogs, are disappearing also.

In the past, hotter days and cooler nights kept the chytrid fungus under control. The disease still killed some frogs, but it didn't kill very many. Pounds believes that with the change in temperature, the fungus spreads more rapidly and over a much wider area. "Disease is the bullet [that is] killing frogs," Pounds wrote. "But climate change is pulling the trigger."

His findings made headline news around the world. Hundreds of newspaper and magazine articles were printed. A few scientists challenged his findings, but most agreed with him.

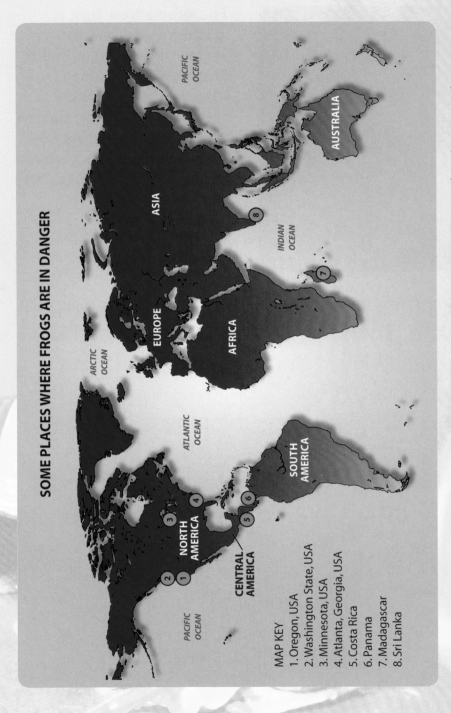

SOME PLACES WHERE FROGS ARE IN DANGER

PACIFIC
OCEAN

AUSTRALIA

ASIA

⑧

INDIAN
OCEAN

⑦

ARCTIC
OCEAN

EUROPE

AFRICA

ATLANTIC
OCEAN

SOUTH
AMERICA

③

④

② ①

NORTH
AMERICA

⑥

⑤

PACIFIC
OCEAN

CENTRAL
AMERICA

MAP KEY
1. Oregon, USA
2. Washington State, USA
3. Minnesota, USA
4. Atlanta, Georgia, USA
5. Costa Rica
6. Panama
7. Madagascar
8. Sri Lanka

Frogs around the world are in danger of extinction. The areas in the map key are discussed in this book.

14

GLOBAL THREATS

Global warming affects frogs in places other than Central America. Scientists have found endangered frogs in other parts of the world.

One discovery was on Sri Lanka, an island off the east coast of India. Scientists noted that many kinds of frogs had disappeared from Sri Lanka within just a few years. Other kinds were in danger of becoming extinct. No one was sure why. The climate of Sri Lanka is a lot like the climate of Costa Rica. The chytrid fungus is widespread in both places. The fungus seemed to be the most likely reason for the frogs' disappearance.

Another discovery was made on Madagascar, an island located east of Africa.

The Madagascar tomato frog is losing its habitat to deforestation. Other frogs on Madagascar died when they could no longer find a cool place to live.

Scientists there believe that at least three kinds of frogs disappeared over a short period of time. As Earth grew warmer, the frogs couldn't stay where they were. It was too hot. They began climbing up the sides of mountains, where it was cooler. As the temperatures continued to rise, the frogs had to keep climbing. Finally they got to the top, but the weather kept getting warmer. With no cool place to go, the frogs died.

Scientists at the University of Oregon studied some types of deformed frogs.

They realized that other types of frogs had disappeared. They blamed intense ultraviolet (ul-trah-VYE-uh-let) **radiation** (ray-dee-AY-shun) from the sun. Called UV-B, this radiation attacks cells in bodies as they develop. It leads to harmful changes in these cells, which kills the frogs or makes them grow in an odd way.

Normally a gas called ozone (OH-zohn) blocks most UV-B rays. Ozone is found

Frogs from Costa Rica, such as the strawberry poison dart frog, are in danger from the chytrid fungus.

Scientists are concerned about the Oregon spotted frog. They estimate that it has lost about three-fourths of its former habitat. One day it may completely disappear from California and parts of Oregon.

high in the atmosphere. Global warming has caused more heat to remain close to Earth, leaving the upper atmosphere colder than before. Ozone breaks up in the colder temperatures, and more UV-B rays are able to reach Earth.

These rays easily go through the thin skin of frogs. If global warming increases, there might be even less ozone. More UV-B rays will get through. More frogs will become deformed or die. They probably wouldn't be the only victims. Higher levels of UV-B rays could also cause a lot of harm to humans and other animals.

The leopard frog is a native to wetlands in Arizona, New Mexico, and northern Mexico. Predators, disease, and human destruction of the land have ruined the homes of more than 75 percent of the leopard frogs.

EXTINCTION

Joseph Mendelson takes care of snakes and frogs at the zoo in Atlanta, Georgia. He is trying to save as many frogs as he can. In 2006, he made four trips to Panama to catch hundreds of frogs that were in danger of becoming extinct.

Chapter Four

THE FUTURE FOR FROGS

Some scientists don't believe that humans are causing global warming. Many others do. They believe the threat that human activity poses to the environment is real—and rising.

Scientists who study frogs are especially alarmed. In 2006, two scientists, Joseph R. Mendelson and Ron Gagliardo, traveled to Panama. The chytrid fungus was killing a lot of frogs there. The scientists frantically caught about 600 frogs. They packed them in special containers lined with moss, then flew back with them to Atlanta, Georgia. They were planning to raise these frogs in places where they could exist safely.

The scientists may have acted in the nick of time. They were sure the frogs they captured would have become extinct within a few months.

Other frogs won't be as lucky. Hundreds of types could become extinct by the year 2050. Some scientists believe that frogs may disappear like the dinosaurs did. Dinosaurs lived on Earth for millions of years. Then they all became extinct in a relatively short period of time. No one knows why. Global warming is one **theory** for their extinction.

Many people believe that global warming is a serious problem. In 1997, most of the world's nations signed the Kyoto Protocol (kee-OH-toh PROH-tuh-kal). A protocol is an agreement. Kyoto is the city in Japan where the agreement was signed.

Under the terms of the agreement, nations would try to reduce the amounts of gases that pollute the air, such as carbon dioxide. However, some people thought the protocol was not strong enough, and that it would not have much impact on global warming. When George W. Bush became president of the United States in 2001, he said the United States wasn't bound by the agreement.

Some people approved of his action. Others disapproved. They said the United States burns more fossil fuel and produces more carbon dioxide than any other country. They believed the protocol would have made a start in reducing pollution.

A flood in San Bernardino County, California, buried the habitat of the mountain yellow-legged frog under ten feet of mud, wiping out the entire population. To scientists' surprise, the frogs reappeared in 2005 after they were thought to be extinct for two years.

Many cities around the world use electric buses, which do not pollute the atmosphere like gasoline-powered vehicles do. Other vehicles called hybrids use both gasoline and electricity. They go much farther on a gallon of gas than conventional vehicles. Hybrid vehicles also produce less air pollution. Another new type of engine uses vegetable oil instead of fossil fuels.

Many people in the United States are taking action to combat global warming. In 2006, California's Governor Arnold Schwarzenegger was setting goals to reduce the production of carbon dioxide and other harmful gases in his state. Greg Nickels, the mayor of Seattle, Washington, has challenged mayors throughout the nation to do the same thing. Major automakers are producing hybrid cars, which run on a combination of gasoline and electric batteries. This combination reduces pollution.

In the meantime, frogs are dying off rapidly. Many scientists are taking the warning seriously. Like the frogs that climbed the mountain, one day humans may find they don't have any other place to go.

Learn as Much as You Can

Ask your teacher or librarian to suggest books and magazines about frogs. You can also find lots of information on the Internet. Then share what you learn with your family and your friends.

Save Energy

Turn off lights, your computer, and the television when you don't need to have them on. You can also help out by riding your bike or walking instead of asking your parents for a ride in the car. When your family needs new appliances, ask your parents to make sure that they are energy efficient.

Plant Some Trees

Trees reduce carbon dioxide in the atmosphere. They can also provide homes for wildlife in your neighborhood.

Recycle

When you go to the store, look for packages with three arrows in a circle. These packages can be recycled. When we recycle, we are conserving natural resources, which helps protect the environment.

What If You Find a Deformed Frog?

If you find a deformed frog or other animal, call your local zoo or college right away. People who work there want the chance to study frogs and other animals that have defects. This helps them find out what is happening in our environment.

Books

Bledsoe, Karen E. *Global Warming*. Logan, IA: Perfection
      Learning, 2004.

Kalman, Bobbie. *Frogs and Other Amphibians*. New York
      Crabtree Publishing, 2005.

Markle, Sandra. *Slippery, Slimy Baby Frogs*. New York: Walker
      and Company, 2006.

Pringle, Laurence. *Global Warming*. New York: Seastar Books,
      2001.

Rockwell, Anne. *Why Are the Ice Caps Melting: The Dangers of
      Global Warming*. New York: Collins, 2006.

Scoones, Simon. *Climate Change: Our Impact on the Planet*.
      Austin, Texas: Raintree Steck-Vaughn, 2002.

On the Internet

The EPA Climate Change Kids Page
      http://www.epa.gov/globalwarming/kids/

Global Warming—Kids page
      http://www.pewclimate.org/global-warming-basics/
      kidspage.cfm

Climate Change for Kids
      http://tiki.oneworld.net/global_warming/climate_home.html

Minnesota Pollution Control Agency
      www.pca.state.mn.us/index.cfm

Zoo Atlanta: Reptile and Amphibian Research
      http://www.zooatlanta.org/research_reptile_research.htm

1896 Swedish scientist Svante Arrhenius describes how gases in Earth's atmosphere retain the heat of the sun.

1954 G. Evelyn Hutchinson, a Yale biologist, states that deforestation will increase carbon dioxide in the atmosphere.

1956 Scientist Gilbert Plass shows how carbon dioxide traps heat and leads to global warming.

1979 The U.S. National Academy of Sciences reports likely temperature rise if carbon dioxide levels increase.

1981 Scientists report that this year is the warmest ever recorded.

1992 The United States is one of more than 100 countries to sign the United Nations Framework Convention on Climate Change. The convention begins to try to slow down climate change.

1997 More than 140 countries sign Kyoto Protocol, which aims to reduce pollution that many believe causes global warming.

1998 Scientists call this year the warmest on record.

2001 The U.S. National Academy of Sciences publishes a report that suggests human actions are a likely cause for the rise in global temperatures. President George W. Bush declares there are problems with the Kyoto Protocol and withdraws the United States from the agreement.

2005 Countries begin observing the terms of the Kyoto Protocol. Scientists call this year the warmest on record.

2006 Scientist J. Alan Pounds publishes a report that says global warming is the reason frogs are dying in Costa Rica. Joseph R. Mendelson and Ron Gagliardo fly to Panama to rescue as many kinds of frogs as they can before the chytrid fungus kills them all.

2007 The Intergovernmental Panel on Climate Change finds that humans are "very likely" the cause of global warming.

BCE

65,000,000	Dinosaurs
50,000	Giant koala
10,000	Saber-toothed tiger, woolly mammoth

CE

1627	Auroch (a mammal similar to cattle)
1681	Dodo bird
1750	Atlantic gray whale
1768	Steller's sea cow
1822	King Island emu
1883	Quagga (a mammal related to the zebra)
1914	Passenger pigeon
1922	Barbary lion
1980s	Java tiger
2006	White dolphin

Cleave, Andrew. *Frogs: A Portrait of the Animal World.* New York: Todtri, 1999.

Maruska, Edward J. *Amphibians: Creatures of the Land and Water.* New York: Franklin Watts, 1994.

Eilperin, Juliet. "Warming Ties to Extinction of Frog Species." *Washington Post,* January 12, 2006. http://www.washingtonpost.com/wp-dyn/content/article/2006/01/11/AR2006011102121.html

Goodman, Brenda. "To Stem Widespread Extinction, Scientists Airlift Frogs in Carry-On Bags." *New York Times,* June 6, 2006. http://www.nytimes.com/2006/06/06/science/06frog.html?ex=1307246400&en=7eadca40d157485d&ei=5088&partner=rssnyt&emc=rss

Handwerk, Brian. "Frog Extinctions Linked to Global Warming." *National Geographic News,* January 12, 2006. http://news.nationalgeographic.com/news/2006/01/0112_060112_frog_climate.html

Morelle, Rebecca. "Climate Culprit for Frog Deaths." *BBC News,* January 11, 2006, http://news.bbc.co.uk/1/hi/world/asia-pacific/4602116.stm

"16 Percent of Frog Species in Sri Lanka May Be Gone, New Survey Finds," *Monga Bay,* July 2, 2005, http://news.mongabay.com/2005/0702-rhett_butler.html

Warrick, Joby. "Mass Extinction Underway, Majority of Biologists Say," April 21, 1998, *Washington Post,* http://www.well.com/user/davidu/extinction.html

EPA: Global Warming: Climate http://yosemite.epa.gov/oar/globalwarming.nsf/content/Climate.html

Frogs an Early Indicator of Global Disaster http://www.solcomhouse.com/frogs.htm

Blakemore, Bill. "Is Global Warming Leading to Extinction?" *ABC News,* July 18, 2005, http://abcnews.go.com/Technology/story?id=942506&page=1&technology=true

Climate Change Milestones http://www.cnn.com/SPECIALS/2005/changing.earth/interactive/timeline/frameset.exclude.html

adapt (uh-DAAPT)—body changes that occur to adjust to changes in the environment.

atmosphere (AT-mus-feer)—the layer of gases that surrounds Earth and makes life possible.

carbon dioxide (KAR-bun dy-OCK-syd)—a heavy gas that is part of Earth's atmosphere.

endangered (en-DAYN-jurd)—in a dangerous situation; at risk of dying out.

extinct (ek-STINKT)—dying out completely; no longer in existence.

fossil fuels (FAH-sul fyools)—things people burn to create energy, such as coal or oil, that are formed in Earth from the remains of dead plants or animals.

fungus (FUN-gus)—a very simple life-form that fastens itself to other living things and takes its nourishment from them.

habitat (HAA-bih-tat)—an area in which a plant or animal lives and grows.

ozone (OH-zohn)—a gas in the atmosphere that shields the earth from harmful rays of the sun.

radiation (ray-dee-AY-shun)—energy such as light or heat that is sent out in rays.

theory (THEER-ee)—a belief based on the study of a number of facts.

INDEX